Hispanic Heritage: Volume 2

Explorers and Conquerors

Richard Sanchez

Published by Abdo & Daughters, 4940 Viking Drive, Suite 622, Edina, MN 55435.

Library bound edition distributed by Rockbottom Books, Pentagon Tower, P.O. Box 36036, Minneapolis, Minnesota 55435.

Photos by:
Bettmann Archive: 9, 11, 15, 17, 19, 21, 23, 25, 28, 29, 30
Archive Photos: 22, 27

Edited by John Hamilton

Library of Congress Cataloging–in–Publication Data
Sanchez, Richard, 1954-
    Explorers and conquerors / Richard Sanchez.
        p.   cm. — (Hispanic heritage ; v. 2)
    Includes bibliographical references and index.
    ISBN 1-56239-332-4
    1. Explorers—Spain—Juvenile literature. 2. Explorers—Portugal—
Juvenile literature.   [1. Explorers.]   I. Title.   II. Series: Hispanic
heritage (Edina, Minn.) ; v. 2.
G279.S26   1994
910'.946—dc20   94-17409
                                                                          CIP
                                                                          AC

CONTENTS

1
INTRODUCTION

The first settlers of what now is the United States came from Asia during the Stone Age. Thousands of years later came a second wave of settlers—from Europe.

But before this second wave could settle here, the land first had to be discovered. Until just 500 years ago, no one in Europe knew it even existed.

It took the daring of sailors from Spain and Portugal to find out about it. They also discovered Central America, South America, the Caribbean Islands and the Philippines—all birthplaces of the Hispanic world as we know it today.

This is the story of their explorations and conquests.

By the dawn of the 1600s, the people of Europe's Iberian Peninsula were rulers of the New World.

2
TWO NATIONS, ONE PENINSULA

Between four hundred and five hundred years ago, Spain and Portugal were the two most powerful nations in the world. They each shared a remote corner of southwestern Europe known as the Iberian Peninsula. This peninsula had a long history of invasion and conquest. The earliest inhabitants were the Iberians. They were attacked by a war-loving people from central Europe known as the Celts. The Celts took Iberian women as their wives and created a new people called Celtiberians.

The Celtiberians were invaded in the 13th Century B.C. by the Phoenicians. The Phoenicians were famous for their ships and ability to navigate the seas. They built colonies and cities in Iberia.

In 480 B.C., Iberia was invaded by the North African empire of Carthage. Next came conquest by the Romans, who drove out the Cathaginians around 210 B.C. Iberia later became one of the leading provinces of Rome. Great cities arose. Culture blossomed. And a language known as Latin came into wide use (Latin is the root of modern Spanish and Portuguese.)

In the 5th Century, warrior tribes from Germany attacked and took over the peninsula by 573 A.D. The German tribes ruled with an iron fist for nearly 150 years before losing most of Iberia to an invasion of Moslems from North Africa in 711 A.D.

These new conquerors were the Moors. They introduced Arabic customs and language along with leather crafts, sword-making, rich architecture and better ways to farm.

Around the 1200s, the few northern Iberian city-states the Moors did not conquer banded together to take back the peninsula. Within 200 years, they had gained enough strength and numbers to almost completely overthrow the Moors. In 1469, Ferdinand II of the province of Aragon married Isabella of Castile. Ten years later, they united their provinces into a single kingdom. Other provinces soon joined them and formed a single, powerful country by then known as Spain.

The only territory that did not join this new nation was located at the far west of the peninsula. This was Portugal.

In the 15th Century, Portugal began to develop a keen interest in sending its ships to faraway places, especially Asia. Asia was a land filled with rare spices, precious medicines, and all sorts of other needed goods. In those days, products from Asia could only be brought in by caravans across the mountains. It was a slow, dangerous journey and very, very expensive to undertake. It was hoped that a sea route would prove faster, safer, less expensive and a lot more profitable.

All this excitement about sailing and prizes for new discoveries helped make Portugal the world's leading sea power. This did not sit well with the people of Spain. Although Portugal was a much smaller nation than Spain, the Spanish rulers feared the Portuguese. A great rivalry between the two countries began. It became a race to rule the world.

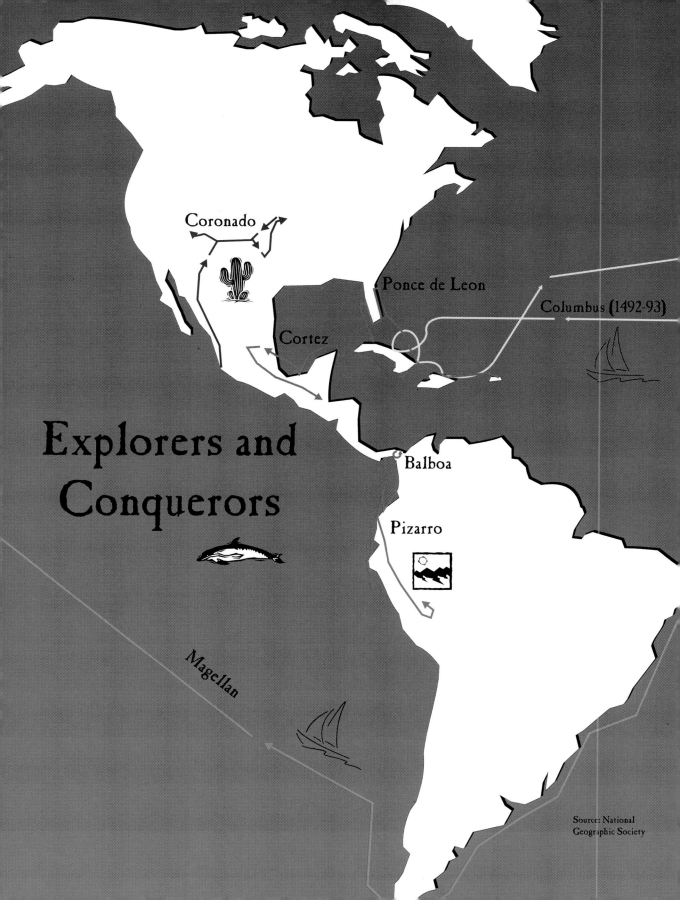

Coronado

Ponce de Leon

Columbus (1492-93)

Cortez

Explorers and
Conquerors

Balboa

Pizarro

Magellan

Source: National
Geographic Society

3
Discovery Of
A New World

For a time in the late 15th Century, it must have seemed as if every young person in Europe dreamed of being the first to find the sea route to Asia. The route was a mystery for a reason. In those days, sailors were just learning how to draw accurate maps. And because no one had ever sailed around the world before, no maps existed that could show the exact shortest way to Asia.

Knowing the shortest possible route was very important. Sailboats back then were tiny compared to ships today. They could not travel very far in one direction because they had room to carry only enough food and water to last the crews a few weeks. Without places along the way to stop for more food and water, everybody on board would die if the ships went beyond their maximum range. And the range could be quite short if the wind blew the wrong way. If that were to happen, the boat might be forced to stay at sea longer than expected. For those reasons, captains did not dare sail very far from land.

Since the world was round, Christopher Columbus believed that the shortest way to get to Asia in the east was to sail west across the Atlantic. He never made it to Asia because along the way he accidentally bumped into the New World.

Around the year 1480, a young Italian adventurer named Christopher Columbus argued the shortest way to get to Asia in the east was to sail due west across the Atlantic. He said this should be possible because the world was round. Of course, scholars and many ordinary people had known for centuries that the world was round—the Greeks had proved it with mathematics long before the time of Christ and even the Bible has references to it. The people of Columbus' day knew that if you traveled west you would eventually end up right back at your starting point because the earth is one big circle.

But the experts didn't think there was a boat anywhere in the world that could sail far enough west to reach Asia before using up all the food and water on board. Columbus thought otherwise. He said the world was much smaller around than others believed. Since it was smaller, the distance across the sea to Asia would be shorter. A good ship should be able to make the voyage without running out of food and water, he said.

Actually, Columbus was wrong about the size of the earth. It was much larger than he thought. The experts he disagreed with were closer to the right answer about the planet's circumference. That's because they had relied on the calculations of the ancient Greeks. Columbus did not.

As a result, Columbus had a hard time convincing any government of Europe to pay for his voyage of discovery. He first asked the king of Portugal. The king said no. Then Columbus went to the king of England who also said no. He next asked the king of France. That king said no, too.

But Columbus did not become discouraged. He kept asking. He was driven by a belief that God had chosen him to make such a voyage so that Christianity could be spread around the world.

Columbus landing in the New World.

Finally, Columbus approached King Ferdinand and Queen Isabella of Spain. They were going to say no. But the queen's treasurer convinced them that they should say yes. Columbus could make Spain very, very wealthy if he succeeded, the treasurer told them.

And so, the king and queen agreed to help Columbus. They gave him three wooden ships named Nina, Pinta and Santa Maria. Columbus sailed from Spain on Aug. 3, 1492.

His convoy sailed west to the Canary Islands where they stopped for food and water. The voyage

11

continued on September 7. The last time they saw land was September 9.

The days turned to weeks and the crews started worrying. It was not that they thought they were going to sail off the edge of the earth. They did not believe any such myth. Rather, they worried about using up the food and water before reaching Asia—or before reaching home in case it became necessary to turn back.

One whole month went by. This was the longest anyone had ever sailed in one direction away from shore. On October 10, the crew was so fearful that Columbus made a promise to turn back if they didn't discover land within the next three days. Then, on the moonlit night before his time was up, they sighted land. A mighty chorus of cheers rose from the decks of the three boats.

The day was October 12. At noon, Columbus arrived on an island he named San Salvador. He was in the Bahamas, but mistakenly thought he had landed just off Asia. It took 30 years of other voyages of discovery to prove Columbus was wrong.

He met friendly natives and stayed only a few days. The crews set sail again and arrived in Cuba two weeks later. Columbus thought Cuba was mainland China. Again he sailed on and came to Haiti, which he named Hispaniola. On Christmas Eve, a storm sank the Santa Maria. The natives of Hispaniola helped rescue the sailors and their cargo. Columbus set sail once more with the Nina and Pinta. He left behind 40 of his men and gave them instructions to hunt for gold.

Upon his return to Spain, Columbus reported his news to the king and queen. They were so pleased that they sent him off on another voyage. This time, they wanted him to bring back gold— lots and lots of gold. So, they gave him 17 ships to carry it back in. Aboard were 1,000 colonists. When they arrived at Hispaniola, Columbus found all the men left behind the year before had been killed by the natives. Columbus' men, it seems, had treated the natives badly. The natives had taken revenge.

During this second voyage and two more after it, Columbus also found his way to Jamaica, Venezuela and Panama.

When Columbus sailed to the New World, he came in three large wooden ships like the one shown here. Their names were the Nina, the Pinta, and the Santa Maria.

4
AROUND THE WORLD

The accomplishments of Columbus set Europe ablaze with excitement. Among the joyful people was a ship's navigator from Portugal by the name of Ferdinand Magellan. He also wanted to try reaching Asia in the east by sailing west, but his own king was not interested in paying for such a voyage. Magellan instead won the backing of the king of neighboring Spain. Magellan was given five ships and 270 men. They left Spain in September, 1519. They were almost out of food by the time they reached the Bay of Rio de Janeiro in Brazil three months later.

The ships then traveled south along the east coast of the mysterious South American continent in search of a way to continue west to Asia. In October, 1520, the ships reached the southern tip of the continent and entered a narrow passage with towering cliffs on either side. This passage led to the Pacific Ocean. Once they entered the Pacific, Magellan sailed west for 98 days. During that time he saw no land except for two desert islands. Just as all hope seemed lost, they arrived at the Marianas Islands. There they found food and fresh water.

They continued, sailing to the Philippine Islands, and then to India, where they soon found themselves in familiar waters. From there they sailed back to Spain. Not only did Magellan reach Asia by sailing west, but he became the first explorer to voyage all the way around the globe.

Ferdinand Magellan was first to sail around the world.

14

5

FOR GOD, GLORY AND GOLD

Directly on the heels of Columbus' first voyage of discovery came soldiers from Spain. These warriors had four jobs. The first was to explore the strange new lands and make maps of them. The second was to find gold and bring it back to Spain. Third was to conquer any and all native peoples and convert them to Christianity. Fourth, establish colonies and create a worldwide empire for Spain. Their motto was "God, glory and gold."

The Portuguese had much the same plan. But Spain had a big head start.

The warrior-explorers from Spain and Portugal were called conquistadors. They were considered the toughest and bravest soldiers in all of Europe. They also could be among the cruelest.

It took only a few thousand conquistadors to defeat the hundreds of thousands that made up the armies of the Inca, the Maya, the Aztec and other native nations. They were able to achieve victory against incredible odds because the Spanish and Portuguese had swords and armor of steel, plus muskets and cannons. The primitive spears and arrows of the natives were no match for the weapons of the invaders.

The Spanish and Portuguese also had another advantage—horses. There were no horses in the New World except for those the conquistadors brought by ship. Mounted on these animals, the Europeans could travel many times faster than the natives who had only their feet to carry them. The horsemen also could swoop down on their enemies and defeat them in combat much more easily.

The natives were very superstitious. They thought the armor, the sword, the gun, the horse and the conquistador were all one creature. This led them to believe they were fighting powerful gods, not ordinary men. They often were so frightened they simply ran away in panic when approached by the conquistadors.

Eventually, the natives realized the Europeans were only men like themselves. They stopped running away. But by then, it was too late to stop the conquistadors from winning.

Each time a native nation or tribe was defeated, the conquistadors took the treasures of gold and melted them down into the shape of little bricks. This was done so that less space would be used inside the boats when carrying the captured gold back to Spain or Portugal.

Meanwhile, the natives who remained alive were forced to work in the gold and silver mines to fetch still more wealth from beneath the earth.

Conquistadors came to the New World to explore new lands, spread Christianity and get rich.

6

FERNANDO CORTEZ

(1485–1547)

The mother and father of Fernando Cortez wanted their son to become a lawyer. But he wanted to be an adventurer. And at age 19, Cortez of Spain sailed to where Columbus had been. He lived in Hispaniola a number of years before resettling in Cuba. By helping crush a rebellion of the natives, Cortez became quite popular with the local Spanish rulers. The governor of Hispaniola was so impressed that he gave Cortez 11 ships and an army of 700 men to explore and conquer Mexico.

Cortez was 34 when he landed on the east coast of Mexico. The year was 1519. There, he founded the city of Vera Cruz.

The men soon complained about the jungle, the insects, and the heat. They wished they could go back to their homes in Spain. This angered Cortez. Fearing his troops would mutiny, he ordered 10 of the 11 ships burned and the remaining one sent back to Spain. Stranded, they had no choice but to finish the job they started.

Cortez left some of his soldiers in Vera Cruz to defend it in case the natives should attack while he and the rest of the troops marched off in search of treasure. A few months later, Cortez and the conquistadors found their way to Tenochtitlan, the capital of the Aztec empire.

Fernando Cortez conquered the Aztec empire in his search for treasure.

HERNANCORTES

Normally, the Aztec would make captives of strangers who approached the city uninvited. Instead, when they saw the lighter-skinned Europeans, the Aztec people bowed to the ground and trembled. Cortez was greeted by no less than the emperor himself, Montezuma.

The reason for this was that Montezuma and his people believed Cortez was their god. Aztec legends long had foretold the coming of a light-skinned god called the Fair God. The Fair God was the chief of all the gods. The Aztec were sure Cortez was this Fair God because he fit the description. More so, Aztec legends predicted the Fair God's coming at almost exactly that particular moment in history.

It was a terrible case of mistaken identity. However, it did not last long. Many of the conquistadors were villains who quickly turned their admirers into enemies thirsting for revenge. Not long after that, the Aztec discovered that these "gods" were in reality ordinary men who could be killed. Montezuma and his generals began plotting their attack against Cortez. But Cortez found out about it and decided to strike first. In no time at all, Cortez captured Montezuma and took from his palace chests full of gold and gems.

About six months later, the Aztec people revolted against both Montezuma and their cruel new rulers from across the sea. Montezuma was killed in the rioting and the conquistadors were driven from the city. Aztec warriors chased Cortez and his men six days through the jungle. Many of the conquistadors were caught and killed. Then, the jungle gave way to an open plain. This was the kind of battlefield the conquistadors favored. They

turned and fought. A tremendous battle took place. The Aztec lost many warriors before they were forced to retreat. The conquistadors limped back to their camp at Vera Cruz.

Cortez visits Montezuma, ruler of the Aztec.

Before tangling again with the Aztec, Cortez talked with the chiefs of several smaller tribes that were neighbors of the Aztec. Cortez convinced the chiefs of these tribes to join him in an all-out war against the Aztec. The chiefs were ready to help. They hated the Aztec because the Aztec had captured many of their sons and daughters over the years to use as human sacrifices.

Now united, Cortez and the natives attacked the Aztec capital. The Aztec fought back hard. The city was surrounded a long time. The people inside could not get out to bring in food and other sup-

The capital of the Aztec empire falls at the hands of Cortez and his conquistadors.

plies. Little by little, they began to weaken from hunger. Eventually, the Aztec warriors could no longer defend themselves well. The city fell into the hands of Cortez.

The neighboring tribes that helped Cortez were happy. The Aztec would never again bother them. But now Cortez was free to attack his friends. One after another, the small tribes were defeated by the conquistadors until, finally, the land belonged to Cortez.

Cortez then became governor of Mexico. In 1536, he continued exploring and discovered Baja California.

7
VASCO NUNEZ DE BALBOA (1475–1517)

Balboa was the first European to see the Pacific Ocean. His life as a Spanish conquistador began in 1501 when he joined a voyage of discovery to the Caribbean Sea. Balboa later settled in Hispaniola. A few years after that, he sailed with an expedition to South America's Atlantic coast.

Several native chiefs there became his friend and they told him of a great sea on the other side of the Andes Mountains in Peru. In 1513, Balboa and 100 conquistadors hiked into the Andes. A few weeks after they started, they reached the top of the mountains. Stretching before them was the Pacific Ocean.

Among the men with him was a scout by the name of Alonzo Martin. Martin went on ahead of Balboa to find a path to the beach. Martin went all the way to the water's edge and became the first European to swim in the Pacific. When the others arrived, Balboa faced the ocean, lifted his sword to the sky and declared in a booming voice that he was formally taking possession of the ocean in the name of his king.

Balboa spent the remaining years of his life as governor of Panama.

Balboa was the first European to set eyes on the Pacific Ocean.

23

8
FRANCISCO PIZARRO
(1470?–1541)

Pizarro of Spain explored the Pacific west coast of South America before conquering the Inca.

He was with Balboa on the expedition to discover the Pacific Ocean in 1513. When Balboa became governor of Panama, Pizarro settled there and ran a cattle ranch. That was in 1519.

But he wasn't happy. He wanted to find gold. So, in 1525, Pizarro led an expedition back along the west coast of South America. He mapped much of Ecuador and came back with a dazzling collection of gold treasures. To Pizarro, this was evidence of the wealthy civilization hidden in the steep Andes Mountains.

Pizarro was determined to find these people. In 1531, he took another expedition to South America and this time searched in Peru. Along the coast, Pizarro came upon many towns in ruins. He learned they had been burned in an Inca civil war.

This civil war started when the sons of Inca Emperor Huayna Capac argued over which of them should wear the crown. Huayna Capac chose

Francisco Pizarro conquered the Inca of South America.

a son by the name of Huascar. When Huayna Capac died, Huascar became emperor. But Huascar's half-brother Atahuallpa wanted to be the supreme ruler of the Inca. Atahuallpa gathered an army and attacked. The civil war went on for a long time. Finally, Atahuallpa won. He ordered Huascar put to death.

Shortly afterward, Pizarro arrived. Word of Pizarro's expedition reached Atahuallpa. Atahuallpa sent men to welcome Pizarro and invited him to visit. Pizarro accepted the invitation.

Atahuallpa was waiting in the Inca city of Cajamarca. To reach it, Pizarro and his conquistadors needed to march through narrow canyons that had steep walls. Looking up as they went, the conquistadors could not help but notice fortress after fortress above them. This made the conquistadors nervous. The Inca in those fortresses could easily rain down deadly spears, arrows and rocks if they wanted.

At last, the conquistadors emerged from the mountain passes and gazed upon beautiful Cajamarca. The tents of the Inca army dotted the landscape as far as the eye could see.

Atahuallpa was impressed when he saw the horses and the Spanish armor. However, he did not believe so small a group of men could be any danger to him.

The next day, Atahuallpa came out to meet Pizarro in the city plaza. Most of the conquistadors had hidden themselves inside the buildings surrounding the plaza. Atahuallpa knew where they were hiding. But he thought they were doing so because they were in awe of him. Soon he learned that the conquistadors wanted to spring a trap on him.

Atahuallpa entered the plaza. He was carried there on a royal litter with 5,000 of his finest warriors beside him. He wore magnificent clothes and a collar made of emeralds. A priest from Pizarro's company stepped forward to present a Bible to Atahuallpa. The emperor looked at the gift in puzzlement. It did not please him. So he tossed it down on the ground.

At that instant, the Spanish came out from their hiding places and opened fire. There was the explosion of cannons. Horses charged through the smoke. Frightened people ran in every direction to escape the flashing swords.

When it was over, thousands of Inca warriors lay dead and Atahuallpa was taken prisoner. The conquistadors cleaned out the entire city of all its gold, silver and copper treasures. Atahuallpa begged for freedom and promised to give the men from Spain a palace full of gold if they would let him go.

Pizarro agreed. Over the next seven months, more than 12 tons of gold treasures had been delivered as ransom. But Pizarro broke his promise and kept Atahuallpa as his prisoner. Finally, Pizarro ordered Atahuallpa executed after he realized the native was no longer of any use to him. In time, Pizarro and his conquistadors took control over all Peru.

Pizarro executed Atahuallpa after he realized the Inca ruler was no longer of any use to him.

27

9
PONCE DE LEON
(1460?–1521)

Ponce de Leon traveled with Columbus on Columbus' second voyage of discovery. De Leon served as governor of the eastern part of Hispaniola. He later conquered Puerto Rico and became its governor in 1510.

The natives he met told him there was an island called Bimini that had a magic fountain. To drink from it, they said, would make an old person young again. De Leon believed that if he could find this fountain of youth it would make him the richest man in the world.

De Leon searched for the fountain of youth in 1513. He never found it. Instead, what he did find was a place he named Florida at the southeast tip of what would become the United States. Eight years later, he tried to set up a colony there but was wounded in a fierce battle with the natives. He was taken by boat to Cuba for medical treatment. He never recovered and died there.

Ponce de Leon searched in vain for the Fountain of Youth.

10
JUAN RODRIGUEZ CABRILLO (1460?–1543)

Cabrillo was the first European to travel up the coastline of California. The year was 1542. Cabrillo was from Portugal but worked for Spain. He started his boat trip in Mexico and headed north. The first place he dropped anchor was San Diego Bay.

From there, he continued north. Cabrillo died during the voyage, but his shipmates kept sailing north. They explored most of the coast of California.

In Spain, the government did not become excited about the discovery of California until word arrived 35 years later that English explorer Sir Francis Drake had tried to claim California for his queen. This made the Spanish rulers fearful of losing California to the English. So, more conquistadors were sent to hold onto the territory. Sebastian Vizcaino was among them. In 1602, Vizcaino began bringing colonists into California as a way to make sure the English were kept out.

Cabrillo explored the California coast, but died on the trip.

29

11

FRANCISCO VASQUEZ DE CORONADO

(1500?–1544)

Coronado was the first European to explore the southwest region of what later would become the United States. He arrived in Mexico in 1535. Coronado heard stories of seven cities made of pure gold somewhere to the north. In February 1540, he led an expedition to try and find these cities.

First Coronado arrived in what now is New Mexico. He found no cities of gold, only the Zuni Indians. Coronado attacked and captured them.

Next, he turned west and explored along the Rio Grande. Coronado wandered up into Arizona, saw the Grand Canyon, and headed into Colorado.

During the Spring of 1541, Coronado journeyed into Texas and Kansas. He returned to Mexico one year later without finding the seven cities of gold.

Coronado searched for the mythical Seven Cities of Gold, but never found them.

12
THE GROWING COLONIES

After Columbus first brought back word of his discovery, Ferdinand and Isabella of Spain made plans to colonize this New World. The conquistadors they sent opened the door to colonization. Before long, colonies were springing up everywhere around the globe.

The Portuguese had similar plans. But Portugal did not act as quickly as Spain. As a result, Spain took the lion's share of discovered lands in the Western Hemisphere. About all that was left for Portugal was Brazil in South America.

The colonies were not easy to run. There was much greed, violence, thievery and hatred among the settlers. But there also were many people who obeyed the law. They wanted justice and fairness for themselves, for their neighbors and for the natives.

One colonial leader who believed in justice and fairness for all was Antonio de Mendoza. He was born in 1490 and was an early governor of Mexico. He also was one of its most successful.

Mendoza was kind to the natives. He spent the colony's money wisely. He built roads for the people to use and he tried to make sure everyone had a job. He brought to Mexico the Western Hemisphere's first printing press.

But for all his goodness, Mendoza could be very stern when people broke the law. For example, in 1541, natives who did not want to worship the way the Spanish priests taught them started a riot. Mendoza was ruthless in the way he restored order.

13
EPILOGUE

By the dawn of the 1600s, the people of Europe's Iberian Peninsula were rulers of the world. Their colonies in North America, Central America, South America, the Caribbean Islands and the Philippines grew and prospered.

Where there were colonists there soon were families. Some husbands and wives were born in Europe, others were born in the New World. Some colonists married natives. Nearly all had children. These are the ancestors of Hispanics today. That is why in our modern United States, the Hispanic heritage embraces people and history from all parts of the world.

GLOSSARY

ARCHITECTURE

Designing a building or using certain types of construction materials so that it looks a certain way when completed.

CIRCUMFERENCE

The distance all the way around a circle.

CIVILIZATION

The highly developed art, science, religion and government of a group of people.

CIVIL WAR

A war between groups of people within one nation.

COLONISTS

People from another nation who have moved to a new land to live and work as a group. They are governed by the nation they left.

CONQUISTADORS

An Hispanic explorer, adventurer or soldier who job it was to find unknown lands and conquer them for his king and queen.

CONVOY

Ships traveling in a group.

CULTURE

The arts, history and activities of a group of people.

EXPEDITION

A long trip to explore a new land.

FORTRESS

A building that has been designed to stand up against attack from enemy soldiers.

LITTER

A special chair carried on the shoulders of a team of people.

MUSKET

An old fashioned rifle that was fired with a spark from a match or a flint. It took a few minutes to reload between each shot. The person using it had to pour an amount of gunpowder down the rifle barrel, pack it down with a long rod and then drop in a marble-size metal ball for a bullet.

NAVIGATOR

The person who plans or directs the way a ship will travel.

PENINSULA

A piece of land surrounded on three sides by water. Its fourth side is connected to a larger piece of land.

RANGE

The farthest distance a ship can travel.

ROUTE

The way to travel from one place to another.

SACRIFICES

A ceremony in which a person or animal is killed as a gift to one or more gods.

WESTERN HEMISPHERE

The half of the earth in which North and South America are located.

BIBLIOGRAPHY

Baity, Elizabeth Chesley. *Americans Before Columbus*. Viking Press. New York. 1961

Kendall, Sarita. *The Incas*. New Discovery Books, New York. 1992.

Lepthien, Emilie U. *The Philippines*. Childrens Press, Chicago. 1984.

Memmi, Albert. *Colonizer and the Colonized*. Orion Press, New York. 1965.

Stuart, Gene S. and George E. *Lost Kingdoms of the Maya*. National Geographic Society, Washington D.C. 1993.

Tuck, Jay N. and Vergara, Norma C. *Heroes of Puerto Rico*. Fleet Press, New York. 1969.

Various contributors. *World Book Encyclopedia*. Field Enterprises, Chicago.

Various contributors. *Encyclopaedia Brittanica*. Encyclopaedia Brittanica Inc., London and Chicago.

INDEX